FIGURES OF HUMOR AND STRANGE BEAUTY

KATH ABELA WILSON

QUITAB EDITIONS

Copyright © 2019 Kath Abela Wilson
Paperback ISBN: 978-1-941783-56-6

All rights reserved: except for the purpose of quoting brief passages for review, no part of this book may be reproduced or transmitted in any form or by any means, electronic or mechanical, including photocopying, recording, or by any information storage and retrieval system, without permission in writing from the publisher.

Cover and Interior Art: Kath Abela Wilson
Author Photo: Tom Clausen
Design & Layout: Steven Asmussen
Copyediting: Linda E. Kim

Quitab Editions: an imprint of
Glass Lyre Press, LLC
P.O. Box 2693
Glenview, IL 60025

www.GlassLyrePress.com

Contents

How to Read *Figures of Humor and Strange Beauty* — vii
Origins — ix

Her Wish — 1
How She Wrote — 3
Journey — 5
Changeling — 9
The Square — 11
Monarchs — 13
The Opening — 15
Hawk — 17
Danger — 19
Gifts — 23
A Slight Accident — 25
Mesa Lane — 27
Spontaneous — 31
Suspense — 33
Her Map — 35
Storm — 39
Pose — 43
Her Book — 47

Archaeology — 53
Publication Credits — 55

The first time I read the first poem aloud to my friend Rick Wilson, he laughed heartily and fell in love. Luckily he loved the rest of the poems too, married me, and we have lived happily ever after. He is my constant accompanist when I read my work aloud, on flutes of the world. I hope you can hear us perform these works together. This is my way of thanking him for his own humor, encouragement, and support. This book is dedicated to him.

How to Read *Figures of Humor and Strange Beauty*

You could have an 18 course dinner party for this book. It might take two evenings. Eighteen guests could prepare a small course, drink, or appetizer to be had after each poem, appropriate to the poem and the sequence in the meal. For the first poem I might suggest a cold sorbet served in a lemon cup or a glass of limoncello. Perhaps with the gift of a stone and an animal cracker.

When I told my friend Lana about this fantasy, she was so enthusiastic she wanted her husband to prepare this meal. I intend to do it as a celebration at home in our Living Room Gallery in Pasadena after this book is published.

But in general, dinner party or not, please don't rush to read this book! I suggest taking at least two years to read through it and savor each of the poems in sequence. They were born that way. It took that long or more for this series to emerge one by one, inexorably, in this exact order and to be polished like sea stones over the twenty years that followed. Each one happened in real time and followed with a strong, sure power and presence at intervals over time.

I asked Lana Hechtmann Ayers, a great poet who understands these things, to write a little comment at the end of my book. The poems are not fantasies. Each happened as described in its own place and time. I could take you on a tour through the places of these poems. I could make a map. Perhaps I will. Consider me your tour guide.

Origins

The poems were written consecutively over three years, during a time in my life when we lived a block from a long wooden staircase that led to a rock strewn shore of the Pacific Ocean in Santa Barbara. Every day I would leave my work for a walk, down the stairs, and found "figures" who seemed to be waiting for me. I photographed as I posed them, often dramatically, against that fantastic backdrop, the various moods and colors of the natural sand, sea and sky in different weathers and times of day. I sketched them quickly in my journal as I went, noting the time and date. A small sampling of these are the illustrations in this book. I always had the feeling I would not live there, be there forever, and I should therefore use this chance as fully as possible while I could.

Most of the "constructions"—simple and emotionally expressive in my mind, these creatures, I returned to the sea they came from. But a few I especially liked, or just spontaneously stayed in my hand on the walk home, are still in our guest room today. Many of the poems were written during those walks, gradually developing from that time and place. Many have a dream-like quality perhaps but none are based on dream. They were all built from actual experience and depict events, sights, sounds and a few memories that were vivid in the present.

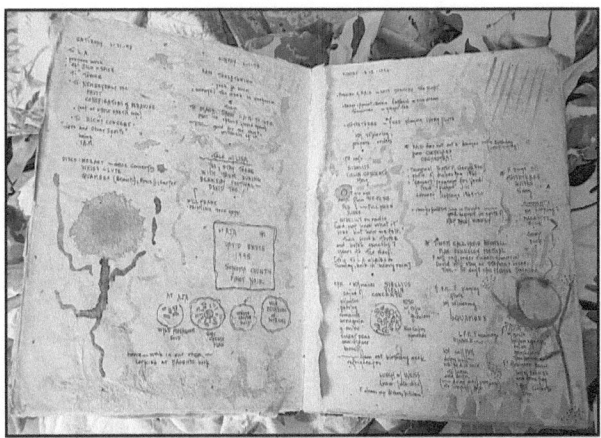

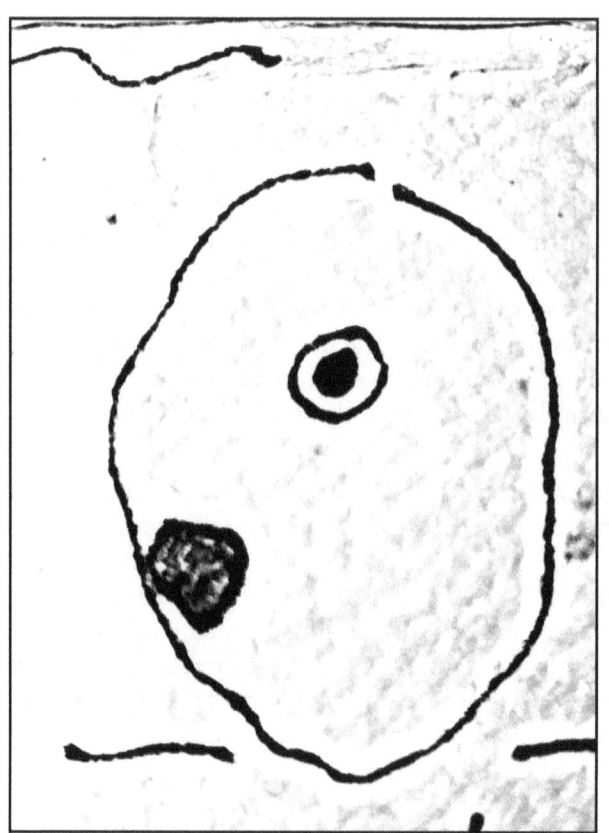

Her Wish
I

At the foot of the stairs

the stones lay in wait.

At first,

she felt the heaviness of their silence.

She held her tongue,

and wished to hear a voice.

Later, she began to carry them home.

They gradually took over her house—

from all the ledges and shelves

they stared down at her,

with their indecipherable markings.

She was charmed,

and wished to understand.

Her third wish came true

when she began to eat them,

one by one.

Luckily, the first was small and light—

and it was when it cracked between her teeth,

that she began to hear them speak.

How She Wrote
II

She looked at the world upside down,

and saw her reflection in the clouds.

On the next day,

she followed with a keen eye

the tracks left

by small stones on the beach.

She lifted each one,

noted its imprint precisely in her book,

and placed it carefully back

in its own spot.

When she returned home,

she rested—

and tired from her tedious work,

she set to dreaming.

When she next looked in her book—

she had written a poem.

Journey
III

She had a flair for excess
that combined with a peculiar sense of direction
to produce, now and again,
exquisite flights of imagination.

It was on one of these journeys,
and as it neared her birthday,
that she bought the airline tickets—
one for herself,
and one for the enormous spool
of white silk cord.

Her mind was like a homing pigeon.
No matter where in its travels it set off from,
it would eventually return
to those key spots in her childhood
where everything began.

She had come to the conclusion,
after visiting these spots
innumerable times in her imagination,

that if a straight line were drawn
from one to the other, in the right order,
an amazing pattern would emerge.
It would be the key to everything.
Now, with her silk cord, she was bound and determined
to find out.

She had planned her arrival for dusk.
The streets would begin to empty,
and she would have the least interference.
Things were remarkably the same as she remembered.
Except they were closer together,
and what she had thought to be hills,
were only slight inclines—
(as is the case on such return trips).

She worked through the night—
walking, tying, and turning.
The white lines sparkled in the moonlight
through the empty streets,
and as the breeze played on them:

the church, the school, the house,
the tree on the hill where she first collected stones,
the wall on which she sat and overlooked the hill.

By the first light of morning her work was done,
when she began to pull the last lines toward her.
The sound of slipping and tightening silk
was interesting and exciting.

***

On the return flight home,
she was not disappointed.
Her arm rested comfortably on the enormous knot
that had so easily formed as a result of her labors.

Always practical, she began to imagine its uses.
Perhaps she could use it as a chair,
it would certainly be comfortable,
and even fit two.
She needed chairs….

Finally, without thinking,
she began to mold it with her fingers
as she always did with things since she was small.
The long neck of a swan began to emerge on one side,
and a fan-like unfolding tail on the other.

As they circled the airport,
she remembered her dreams.
They had all been sweet ones on this journey,
which for all its twists and turns
and long windedness,
she judged a fine success:
she was flying back to the friends that she loved
with a good story, she thought.
She closed her eyes and imagined
how their eyes would light up as she told it.

Changeling
IV

She watched, fascinated—

his bare feet adhering to the ceiling,

as he walked toward the beautiful white door

with its high doorknob

that it seemed one should struggle to attain.

He glided along easily

and floated in, naked

lit with golden light.

After he closed the door,

she bathed in the glow

that streamed from the gap above

to where she lay

sideways on her bed,

her chin tipped upwards.

With dreamlike precision

she knew—

nothing would ever be the same.

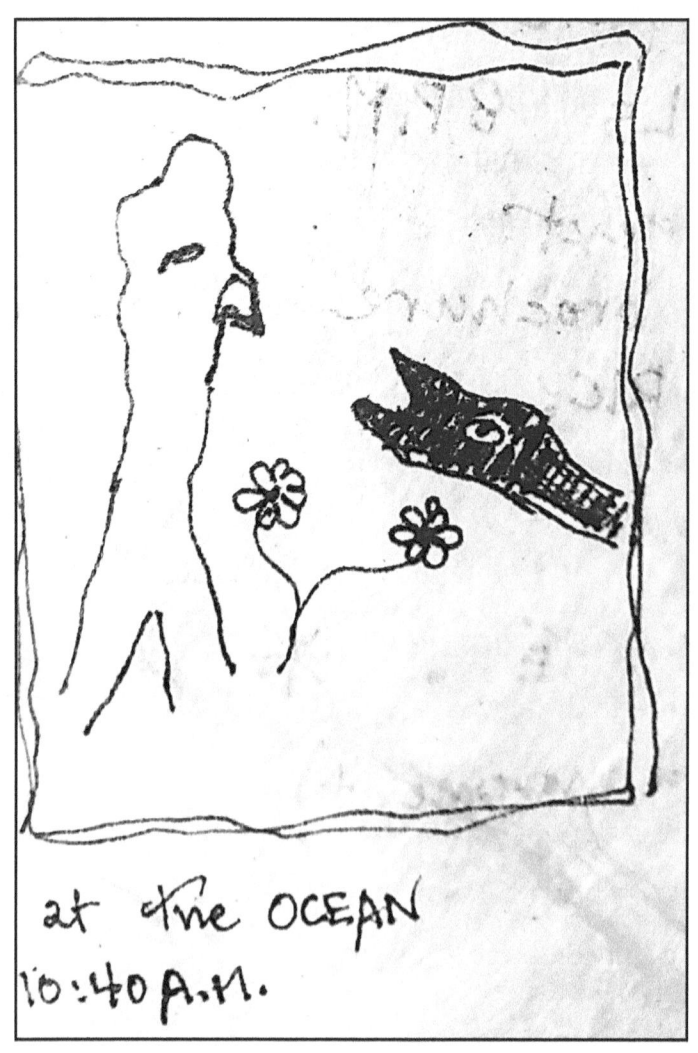

The Square
V

Circling the square,

she found its center with her eye,

and made her way to it

in a straight line,

with more than her imagination.

How easily her arms pushed off the surface

(a bright blueness mixed with white).

A certain giddiness set in, as her feet

grazed a soft greenness above,

and seemed to stick there,

along with the trees.

She had taken her walk, pen in hand,

quickly around and through the square,

but had not written a word.

She was returning on time.

She reached for the doorknob,

but looked back, longingly, over her shoulder—

to where she had come from.

She saw colorful leaves
float gently down in the empty square,
and slowly moving clouds, long and white,
were silent before her eyes.

Breathless, she watched one last cloud change,
a graceful gliding that caught her admiration.
She recognized her journal:
serene, unreachable;
its accordion white fan opened out
and extended lightly and invitingly,
back—into the blue.

Monarchs
VI

It was a day for crossing the shadows
of birds, she noticed as she walked.
She sat on the ocean, facing the beach,
leaned backwards, and floated out
across the channel.
She touched the islands gently with her fingertips,
then stood (feet upward)
and eased over the islands backwards.

From the other side,
the sight of the clear blueness
made her feel at home.
Before her—ocean and sky, unobstructed
as far as she could see.

Suddenly she turned.
In the distance, on the beach,
standing beneath the shadow
of a solitary large bird
(riding the wind, hovering)
she saw herself.

It was the time of many monarchs—

and as one flew by lightly

(orange across the shadow)

it broke her spell.

She walked up the stairs,

away from the beach,

and back to her home.

The Opening
VII

It was the hottest and quietest day of the year.

She sat with him

on the stone step

outside a white, small house.

They had been there for hours already,

acknowledging to one another

with a soft glance or raised eyebrow,

variations in the small but distinct sounds.

Not the slightest crack

went unnoticed, for each was a sign of opening.

In spite of their differences,

here they were at one:

in the sounds of the wind

that spoke out of the shells

in the pines above,

and in the patterns made

by the seeds and the slight husks

that fell on the stone path before them.

After the heat of the day

began to diminish,

and as night fell,

they stood and turned,

then slipped together

into the silence

between sounds,

through the white open door

to dream.

Hawk
VIII

It seemed to come to her in a dream—

the body of the hawk

was covered with hieroglyphics.

White against auburn,

they glistened in the sunlight

that filtered through the trees

to the branch over the creek.

They reminded her of a favorite stone

she had found in the sand months ago.

At that moment she gazed

into the eyes of the hawk:

still, intense, patient.

She imagined herself floating

into a deep canyon—

the red-brown walls

were covered with rows of fine white markings.

She was exhilarated as she moved

in one long breath,

through the air slowly, across and down,

and as she did, the signs began to resemble faces:

long and noble,

and each had a mouth that was a door

made of interesting old wood

with metal fixtures,

and each felt inviting as she passed—

as if to enter any one of them

would be to know the answer

to some question.

Danger
IX

As she walked,
she averted her eyes.
She knew that with her mood as it was,
if she looked too closely at anything—
it would turn into a poem.

For once she would be responsible
for everything.
There had been a week
of hot clear days
when things had been all too visible.
Everything was dry;
ready to crack open,
like those pine cones
that were popping seeds
all over her doorstep.
She already had enough poems in her head—
and not enough time to write them down.

The weather was cooperating.
A rich wet mist was collecting in the air,

dimming the outlines of things,

giving her respite,

and everything else a rest

from jumping out at her

with vivid clarity.

She had reached the stairs,

and she was relieved to see

that the islands were obscured.

Even the ocean was indistinct.

As she descended the stairs, she hesitated.

It was the lowest tide she had ever seen.

Literally thousands of stones

were strewn temptingly along the shore.

She was determined to keep her eyes to herself,

and watch her own footsteps.

Tracks of unseen birds led to the ocean and disappeared.

She had walked a short distance along the beach,

and begun to walk back toward the stairs when she saw it:

it was as if the cool white mist had congealed

into one white crystalline stone.

She felt the wind rising

as she picked it up.

She moved it through her fingers

and as she gazed out to sea—

she knew it was a sail.

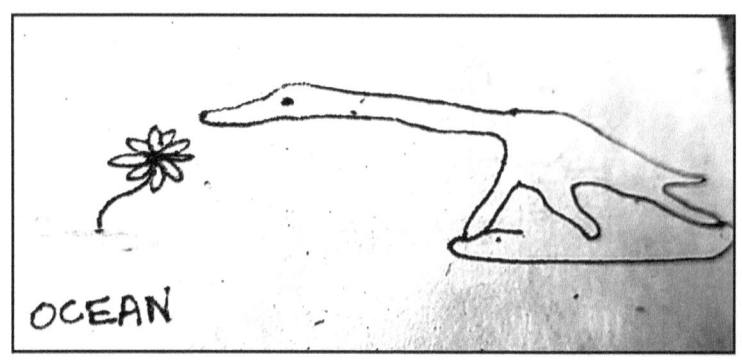

Gifts
X

"She's out!"
He had to shout with good humor
over the clamor of poems in her head.
She was beginning her walk,
and he was saying goodbye at the door.
As soon as her legs started moving,
the poems began.
The words, as they clacked together,
were the sound of beach stones
scattering on the shore.

"A visit to my friends,
and then to the ocean," she thought.
On their outdoor table two stones
had jumped out at her yesterday,
right into the middle of her poem.
The tempting memory
of their small light animal shapes
fed her imagination.

"They're yours!" said her friend
in answer to her inquiring look.
"We found them for you on our trip."
She relished the thought,
but was puzzled along with them
at how one had cracked
open at the mouth
since their return.

On her way home
she walked along the shore.
In the soft underwater clatter
of the rising tide
she found the rest of her poem.
She could not remember
biting the stone,
but when he kissed her
as she came in,
he noticed that she was strangely quiet,
and her lips were salty.

A Slight Accident
XI

"New steps to the beach,"
she thought.
It was a sudden realization
as the wind had come
and taken the fan-like pages of her unfolding book
down toward the blueness beneath.

She had hold of its cover,
but she saw it sway,
cloudlike, toward the sea.
It seemed almost to disappear.
Her head was full of the sound
of the rising tide,
and she felt that she too might vanish.

It was the sound of her own writing
that woke her from her blank reverie.
She saw faint black tracks
fade into the distance…
Small graceful marks,
freshly made, climbed up and down

the whiteness, and seemed

to know where they were going.

For hours she stood, between the sky and the sea,

gathering and folding

the pages back into themselves

and then

into the blue covers that held them.

Mesa Lane
XII

First lines

sprang into her head

and fell at her feet.

She walked on the long strips of bark

discarded by the trees.

This was the street that she lived on,

and she walked there every day.

She had felt for a long time,

that it had been built by someone

as a great poem.

It was a magnificent conception,

and humorous too, she thought—

a poem she could walk into;

cars even drove through it

on either side of the long straight line

of tall, wide trees.

She felt the space around her

full of activity.

Words leapt from her mind,

and scattered as she went.
At her feet the crisp pods
exuded the strong scent of eucalyptus.

On her many walks
she counted and recounted the trees,
as if she were remembering dreams—
fixing them in her memory.
The pattern of their planting
filled her imagination.

The two or three shorter ones
changed her count every time,
and strangely interrupted the long thick strokes
toward the sky.

Where there were gaps
she stopped,
and listened to her own breathing.

There were two

out of line at the end

which she never knew if she should count.

They stood apart from the rest

like sentinels—watching over the place

where the poem leaves off,

and the ocean, with its loud voice

begins.

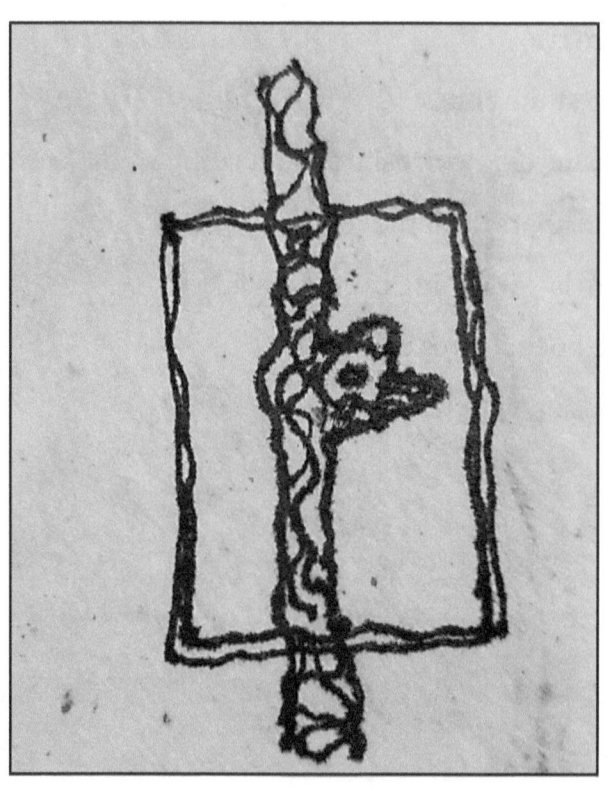

Spontaneous
XIII

She placed a white stone
at the foot of the small red maple.
She had found it on the beach,
round and as heavy as she could hold
in one hand as she walked.

It was a brilliant solution, she thought,
anyone might guess that she had it in mind from the beginning.
It was a spontaneous last gesture
before nightfall,
just before she entered her house,
at the end of her walk to the sea.
She only vaguely knew whose tree it was,
but she was sure they would not notice,
or if they did, might wonder, but not move it.
It would always be there for her.
That night she dreamed.

The moon rose and glistened against the sky.
Through the crystal white glow
at the foot of the tree
she disappeared into the beginning
of her poem.

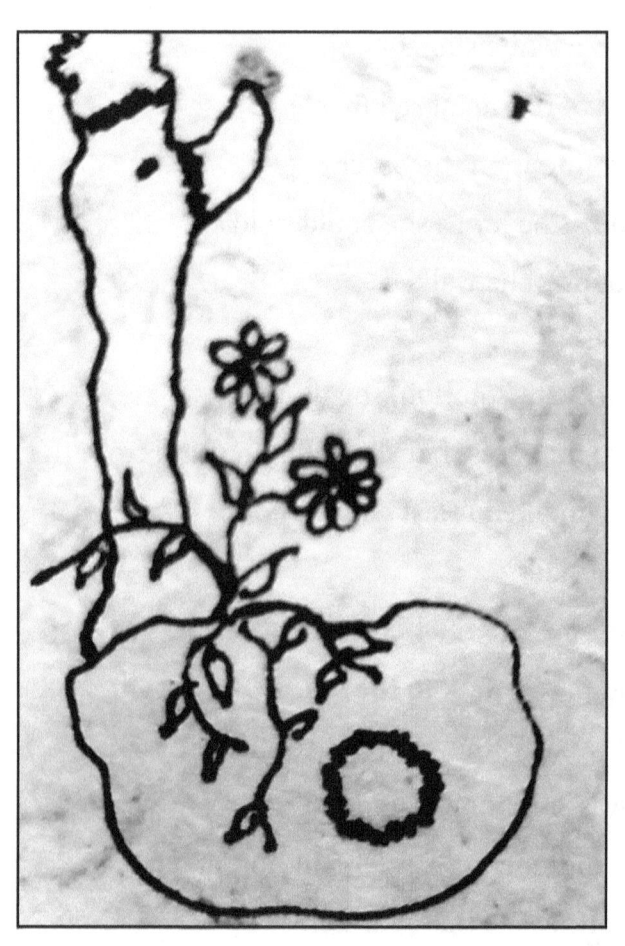

Suspense
XIV

In her dream she slept
in the thin curved cup of the moon,
and the reflection of the earth
was upon her.
She saw herself
among the friends that walked together
along mountain's rim
to the highest point, at end of day,
then stopped and stared over the edge—up
into her eyes.
For the time, their city was erased.
They had stepped into her dream ongoing,
of gold and white, slow moving silence.

Then different, and yet the same,
they slid into a stream of light that carried them.
Her thoughts became stars,
their hearts became trumpets;
sweet and clear tones bloomed into the night.
Held in suspense
—their lives—
were their accompaniment.

Her Map
XV

It was a startling discovery.
She looked back into her past,
and saw herself
moving through an immense tableau.
It surprised her that all these years
she had not noticed.

There were gaps in her experience—
times when she would stop and stare
and often write a poem
that would have nothing to do
with that time or place.
Later when she read it,
the words were a key
that unlocked her memory
of the smallest detail of those moments.
She saw herself in her pose,
and the objects around her
returned with the clarity
of her favorite dreams.

Only recently had she begun to rearrange things.

First she had placed a white stone
at the foot of a small red-leafed tree.
Now, she watched critically
the fall of a single leaf,
and noted the position into which it fell.
When a small purple flower with golden center
poked its head up alone
through the grey iron grillwork bridge she crossed,
she smiled approvingly.

What grew or was scattered
was part of her tableau.
She watched with interest,
and with dreamlike assurance,
moved things,
making distinct but subtle changes
spontaneously, and with a natural sense of ease.
She noted them carefully in her book,
and began to move through her tableau
with a sense of familiarity and recognition.
It was a dream she could return to,
to adjust, to reshape

on her walks to the sea.
The colors and forms that she had chosen
moved her imagination
and in the dark before dream
her memory became a map.
She visited the sites of her constructions
each in turn—
until with a sudden hush,
she would step into the world she had created,
as once a white heron
delicately stepped into her poem:
into the silence of a sunlit garden,
into the stillness of late afternoon,
into the sound of a fountain spilling over—
and her eye was its eye,
serene and slow.
A feather curved and trembled
in her tableau.
She watched
for the smallest breath
of inspiration.

Storm
XVI

As far as she could see before her
into the distance
the sky and the ocean were the same.
The clouds rolled in waves into the sea,
the sea was furious against the shore.
It rose and turned to clouds—
white and wet against her face.
She walked between storms and found
her poetic landscape
utterly changed.

In the midst of her poem
five trees had fallen during the night;
their thick trunks lay silent
across her path to the beach.
The dark silhouettes of their roots
torn upward toward the sky
took on the shape of creatures in conversation.
She listened closely for words
buried in the earth
with the lifetimes of the trees.

On the faces of the rough stone cliffs
that looked out toward the sea,
she had left her signature.
She had built there a gallery of her works.
She chose from what the ocean left her:
color and form, branch and stone.
She moved them in her tableau,
and then the ocean moved them.
Now it had taken them back.

In the blank space
she stood and stared
out into what had been the blue.

It was then that she heard a voice.
It was not the sound of small stones chattering.
She shivered as the ocean drew in its breath—
and the large rocks beneath
shifted, moving against each other
with each crashing wave.

On her walk home
her mind was quiet.
When she came to the tree
by which she had placed one white stone, she stopped and smiled.
"Back to the beginning," she thought.
Above the stone the small tree was bare.
Beneath it, the dark earth had receded.

She did not touch the stone,
but in her dream,
she held it to her ear.
Simultaneously spoken
were all the words of her poem—
and as she listened
she looked
as far as she could see before her
into the distance.

Pose
XVII

Was it not her, but another

who stood in that attentive pose

beneath the tree

near the top of the stairs

that led to the sea?

She held her breath:

one arm out straight,

eyes closed,

then pressed her palm

flat against the tall eucalyptus,

fingers pointing upwards—

as if to feel a pulse,

as if to leave a mark.

She listened.

Was it the end of her last poem

that came to her through the long silence?

Dark lines that came in waves,

repeating, turning white,

they were the cloud

that carried her.
She felt a sudden stillness sink
as if the birds that filled the treetops
over which she moved
fell silent and in daylight went to sleep.
She walked the fine line along the edge
of multiple awakenings
that rose and spread
along the shore to disappear.
She became a wing
that brushed against the window
where she slept
in interlocking dreams enfolded.

With open eyes she heard again the sea—
or was it a voice that came to her
through the dark channel between days,
as a prelude, flutelike, resounding
with words she did not know?

They came to her

in long white diagonals towards the shore.

It was in that moment

that she found herself

walking away from the tree

awake, pen in hand,

in the midst of her next poem.

Her Book
XVIII

There was a certain ecstasy

to the uprising that gave her voice.

She felt it in the air around her,

and in the long saturated earth.

The winter rains had been intense.

the storms had raged beyond their season.

Now she was crossing the bridge

into a world that was the result of such excess.

This was her poem.

She created as she walked

one long line through the overgrowth of flowers.

It was her path to the sea.

From the overwhelming debris

each day she posed one solitary shape

of wood or stone at ocean's edge

against the sea and sky.

Figures of humor and strange beauty—

she created them with her eye,

their singular gestures

caught in that moment before speech,

poised before the ocean's indrawn breath,
about to disappear.

In the afternoon light
she saw her favorite rock
further along the shore.
She walked quickly toward it in the rising tide,
knowing her back fit perfectly into its curves,
anticipating the rise and fall
of syllables that would absorb her
and the space between waves
where words would be the spray
that moved her.

She posed herself
As she had posed the others.
The tide rose.
The sun slipped into the sea
as it painted her silence.
She was alone on her rock
that seemed to drift out

amidst the deepening water.

She glanced back to where she had walked…
On that narrow beach
(as if fallen flowers
had upsprung to bloom again)
her creatures gathered, in simultaneous return,
each to its place, mouths open, gesturing
toward one another and the sea.

Released, invoked,
she did not move, but seemed to join them.
They had gone beyond speech, become one voice
that came through them as a roar,
as if from a distance.

She looked once more:
there was an empty beach.

She turned and gazed.
The ocean had become a blank page

alive with gold sparks glimmering
as if with creatures in constellations
beneath the surface, where they stirred again.

She relaxed into stone curves
and listened
as if to what was read aloud.
Continuously turning
transparent pages
spread over her lightly.
She breathed
between waves of words
and heard the whispers
of their torn edges against the shore.

Immense above:
the sky, awash with stars.
She watched until one,
with bold stroke, fell
from sky to sea,
And in its flash—

she saw herself

on her rock.

She was

an illumination

in her own book.

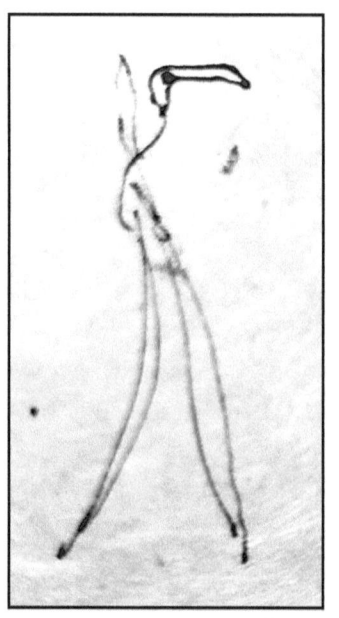

Archaeology

It is fascinating to suddenly find yourself your own archaeologist looking into and under the objects that you have kept. It is especially interesting when they are literary and underlie the poetic process of your own life. I find myself doing this now twenty years after the inception of these poems. I am still alive, living with these objects, moving them around and examining them. In a sense I am a cliff dweller, third floor of a condo where I have collected remnants of my own past. I became unexpectedly married to a friend who heard them and witnessed some of the figures being born. In fact I am living in the house he lived in, where I visited and created in the end the final draft of the last of these poems, *Figures of Humor and Strange Beauty*. I had indexed the fragments I had written over a year in several of my own large writing and sketching journals, all aimed at this last poem #18. But that is another story.

Just a few months ago before I started working on digging through my journals for the origins, fragments, texts and sketches made during this poetic series of twenty years ago I had a dream and recorded it in a small story form called "cherita." I published it a few weeks ago in a new British poetry journal called *ephemerae*:

in the second hand store

surprised by familiar objects
dream journals

handwritten and drawn
treasures a colorful life
of someone who used to be me

Publication Credits

A few of these poems have been previously published.

"Her Wish" *Pirene's Fountain, 10th anniversary edition,* November, 2018

"Changeling" as tanka prose, titled "How She Changed" *Bright Stars #3,* Keibooks, 2014

"Hawk" as tanka prose, titled "Her Reverie" *Bright Stars #3* Keibooks, 2014 (It seemed to come to her in a dream)

"Storm" titled "Between Storms", *Scryptic Vol 1:2,* 2017

"Suspense" *Altadena Poetry Review,* Anthology 2018

Glass Lyre Press

exceptional works to replenish the spirit

Glass Lyre Press is an independent literary publisher interested in technically accomplished, stylistically distinct, and original work. Glass Lyre seeks diverse writers that possess a dynamic aesthetic and an ability to emotionally and intellectually engage a wide audience of readers.

Glass Lyre's vision is to connect the world through language and art. We hope to expand the scope of poetry and short fiction for the general reader through exceptionally well-written books, which evoke emotion, provide insight, and resonate with the human spirit.

Poetry Collections
Poetry Chapbooks
Select Short & Flash Fiction
Anthologies

www.GlassLyrePress.com

www.ingramcontent.com/pod-product-compliance
Lightning Source LLC
Chambersburg PA
CBHW030133100526
44591CB00009B/631